AFTER MIDNIGHT—
BEFORE DAWN

A play
DAVID CAMPTON

SAMUEL   FRENCH

LONDON
NEW YORK TORONTO SYDNEY HOLLYWOOD

CHARACTERS:

Old Woman
Neat Woman
Man (or Embittered Woman)
Girl (or Simple Young Woman)
Boy (or Frightened Young Woman)
Calm Woman

The action takes place in a prison cell, just after midnight

Time—late sixteenth or early seventeenth century

PRODUCTION NOTES

Although the play was originally produced with a mixed cast, it could be staged with an all-female cast as indicated, with very slight changes to the text.

When the Man strikes the Calm Woman, and when the Neat Woman and the Boy kick her, the blows should not actually land on the body; if delivered with shouts of fury, the right impression will be given.

The door in the set is not practical. The step in front of the window is optional (in the original production it was a 12-inch high rostrum), but it raises the Calm Woman to a commanding position during the opening scene when she is not speaking. If a rostrum is not available, another bench could be used.

AFTER MIDNIGHT—BEFORE DAWN

A seventeenth-century prison cell

Moonlight streams through a barred window on to six manacled prisoners

An Old Woman on her knees is huddled in an attitude of prayer, mumbling unintelligibly. A lumpish simple-minded Girl in her late twenties is curled up in straw trying to sleep. A middle-aged Man sits on a bench with his back to a wall, face hidden in hands. A Woman in her thirties sits upright in the middle of the floor, staring into space as though in a state of shock. She is possibly more neatly dressed than the others, having striven to keep up appearances in difficult circumstances. A Boy in his late teens lies face downwards, whimpering. A Woman in early middle-age stands by the window from which she can just see out. Alone among the occupants of the cell she seems untroubled, calmly waiting. The Old Woman's prayers become briefly audible

Old Woman God ha' mercy. Lord ha' mercy. Saints ha' mercy.

Neat Woman (*in a monotone*) It was a mistake. They should admit their mistakes.

Old Woman Mercy, God. Mercy, Lord. Mercy . . .

Neat Woman They meant to take somebody else. Not me.

The Boy's whimpering becomes louder. The Girl stirs and sits up

Old Woman God save us. Lord save us.

The Man looks up

Man Stop your caterwauling, you sop-witted bezoms. Nothing's going to save us.

The Boy gives a cry of terror. The Girl shuffles over to him

Girl Don't fret, lad. (*She puts a hand on his shoulder*)

Boy (*wincing*) Ah!

Girl Back sore?

Boy (*looking up*) I—I . . .

Girl Perhaps I'm more used to a strapping than you. Mistress
were always over fond of laying about her when mispleased.

Boy I—I didn't cry out.

Girl Not you.

Boy Not then. Not even when they . . . (*He buries his face against
her shoulder*)

Girl There, there.

Neat Woman Why should they beat on my door? I always kept
myself apart. Nobody heard me spreading tattle. I scarcely
spoke, except to my Tib.

Girl There, lad. (*She puts her arm around him, but touches a sore
spot again*)

The Boy winces and pushes her away again

Girl Sorry.

Boy To loosen my tongue. A touch of pain now, they laughed,
to mind me of hell-fire later. Then they showed me instruments.
Oh.

Neat Woman Someone must have spread tales.

Boy Hot irons and pincers.

Girl Be thankful it's over, lad.

Boy Over.

Girl No more beady-eyed crows with questions, questions . . .

Boy Give thanks because . . .

Neat Woman I was stirring the broth when they broke in. I
showed them the mutton, the onions, the turnips, the herbs . . .
But still they called it Hell's Brew.

Boy There's a device for stretching a person. It isn't even con-
sidered persuasion. Words from the rack count as free con-
fession.

Girl I yelled at their ugly great needles—screamed worse than
the old sow when her farrow were taken. But when I stopped,
so did the pricking. If I'd known that were what they wanted,
I'd ha' clamped my teeth shut long afore.

Boy They only had to explain the purposes of the machine, and
I babbled like a stream in spate. (*He breaks down and cries*)

Neat Woman Everybody drew aside on from the path when I

was taken. What could they find to whisper? A mistake had been made.

Girl Poor boy.

Boy Lies. Lies. I had naught to do with the powers of darkness.

Girl Who has?

Boy Yet I confessed.

Girl Why shouldn't you? If you spoke after your limbs had been torn apart, all that agony would have been for naught.

Boy I confessed to abominations. Had I danced naked before the devil's altar? Yes. Had I kissed his backside? Yes. Had others been with me? Yes. Who? Yes. Names. Yes. Lies. Lies. But yes. Yes. To anything. Yes. Yes. Yes.

Neat Woman I shouldn't be in this place. It's not just.

Man Bleating for justice?

Old Woman Justice, Lord. Give us justice.

Man You'll get justice on Judgement Day. Not until.

Boy With every "yes" I knotted the hemp around my own throat.

Girl We're not so deep in the midden as you fear.

Boy How can you smile? You'll hang, too.

Girl Hang?

Boy Yes, hang.

Girl Why should I hang?

Boy You heard the judge pronounce sentence.

Girl Old Rumbleguts with the black kerchief over his wig? Did all those words mean that I should hang?

Boy With us. Tomorrow. Tomorrow.

Old Woman Spare us, Lord. Spare us, sweet Jesus.

Girl We've done naught to be hanged for, lad.

Man At a rope's end innocent swing as dead as guilty.

Girl I can't bring my mind to hanging.

Man No more than a cow imagines a butcher.

Boy By this time tomorrow we'll be rotting in the cold earth. Cold. Cold! (*With a cry he covers his face*)

Neat Woman I have done nothing to bring me here.

Man Avarice brought me here. Malice and murdering greed. Prosperity's a crime in these times. A person can't enjoy the fruit of their labours without a charge of being about the devil's business. Your neighbours sell more cloth than you or their cow yields more milk?—have them put away. Envy's the crime, not witchcraft.

Old Woman Deliver us from evil. Deliver us, Lord.

Neat Woman I am no witch.

Man Is any one of us? If we were witches, would we be here? The devil looks after his own.

Calm Woman (*by the window*) Full moon in a cloudless sky. There'll be frost before morning.

There is a pause. Suddenly aware of her presence, one by one the others turn to look at her. Even the praying Old Woman pauses

There's a cart by the gate. What will its next load be?

Girl Turnips maybe.

Calm Woman A fine turnip you'll make.

Girl The cart's for us?

Calm Woman A short life and a merry one. With a crowd to cheer while you dance.

Girl Will they throw pennies, too?

Man She means dance on air, you witless cowpat.

Girl On air? I've never done that before.

Man Nobody does it but once.

Girl Hear that, lad? We're to dance on air. Will you partner me?

Calm Woman I've seen the hangman at work. A master of his craft. And he's had plenty of practice lately.

Boy I can't die. I mustn't die.

Girl Who spoke of dying?

Calm Woman Who needs to? But the rope's ready.

Girl There's to be no whipping, is there?

Calm Woman Nobody will whip you again.

Girl You don't know the mistress. She'll be angered that I've been away so long.

Calm Woman Sweet innocence. I do believe you'll forgive the executioner.

Man You'll not smile so smug when your eyes are bulging.

Calm Woman Few are vouchsafed precognition. But I am assured a rope does not figure in my end.

Man You were condemned with the rest of us.

Calm Woman Aye.

Man But you'll not swing with us?

Calm Woman Should I?

Man You've influence with Higher Authority.

Calm Woman Call it so.

Man Delusion.

Neat Woman They may discover their mistake. Time yet. A little. Do you believe . . .?

Calm Woman Indeed. But your faith's not my faith.

Neat Woman We are innocent.

Calm Woman Of what?

Boy I confessed, but I lied. There was no dancing at full moon. There was no sacrificing at heathen altars. I only told them what they wanted to be told. Lies. °

Calm Woman What, did you never fly on a broomstick?

Boy Never.

Man Did you?

Calm Woman Never.

Neat Woman You are as innocent as the rest of us.

Old Woman Holy Mary. Blessed Saints . . .

Calm Woman You're praying to the wrong quarter, grandmother. Would you expect the blessed saints to turn you back from the very threshold of Heaven? What's a few minutes' gasping compared with eternal bliss?

Man You have petitioned your Higher Authority, of course?

Calm Woman Of course.

Man The Lord Chief Justice is to intervene on your behalf?

Calm Woman My Lord will have his way.

Man Come down in person and open the prison gates for you, eh? Or at the last minute pluck you from the cart.

Calm Woman I do not know how his will is to be manifest. I only know that I shall not die on the gallows.

Man One of the saved, are you?

Calm Woman One of the damned.

Man Damned?

Calm Woman As you so rightly concluded— The Devil looks after his own. (*She turns again to the window*)

Neat Woman The devil?

Calm Woman The moon almost kisses the earth. His arm will be strong tonight.

Old Woman Lord protect us. Saints protect us.

Man She'd sell her soul for a cheap jibe.

Calm Woman A higher price than that.

Girl Have you truly seen the devil? What does he look like?

Calm Woman With a master such as mine some reticence is necessary.

Neat Woman Folly. Rumours begin with such mindless prattle. Then the evil spreads. Loose tongues brought me here.

Boy Will the devil take you hence?

Calm Woman Why should I invite mockery from unbelievers?

Man Aye. Hold your peace. We've misery enough without the torment of clacking tongues.

Calm Woman So be it.

Man We all die tomorrow. All. All.

Neat Woman All.

Boy Not me. Not me.

Man All.

Girl Don't trouble yourself so, lad. Dying's natural. Many's the time I've wrung a chicken's neck. One twist and it's over.

Boy No!

Man (*furiously*) You're a clod, girl.

Girl I meant dying's peaceful like. The other week I found a dead rabbit. He might have been sleeping. I'd have taken him for the pot, only when I stirred him, his belly was full of maggots.

Man Shut that cess-pit of a mouth before I shut it with my fist.

Calm Woman Bravely spoken. A worthy match for a milkmaid.

Girl I'm no child. See my arm. I've had men on their backs.

Calm Woman Strange reversal.

Man I won't be drawn into a brawl on account of a snivelling brat.

Boy I'm no worse than you. You're all cowards. All afraid.

Calm Woman Yet you fear the devil more than you fear death.

Old Woman Our Father which art in Heaven . . .

Calm Woman How odd those words sound . . .

Old Woman Eh?

Calm Woman In that order.

Old Woman Are you—truly—one of—them?

Calm Woman Them?

Old Woman A witch.

Calm Woman Say I struck a bargain with one who is all powerful. A scrap I weighed as lightly as a cast-off clout for the benefit of that power.

Man Power? What power? Chains and fetters hold you as

secure as they hold that old mumbler. Will you use those powers to dull the agony when the noose bites into your neck?

Calm Woman I repeat—I shall not be hanged. Terms were agreed. A service on my part in return for a service on his.

Neat Woman What—service?

Calm Woman Have you a wish to trade?

Neat Woman I—I don't believe in such—superstitions.

Girl If you have powers, lady, show us.

Calm Woman Ribbands out of air? Vanishing eggs? I'm no conjurer. If you want magic seek out a fairground mountebank.

Girl What other powers are there?

Calm Woman Over hearts. Over minds.

Man Over locks and bolts would be more use.

Calm Woman I shall convince you yet.

Man When?

Calm Woman When I escape the executioner.

Boy How? How can that be done?

Calm Woman There's a contradiction. You ask how a thing can be done, yet you don't believe that it can be done.

Boy I believe. I believe.

Calm Woman You believe a drowning man can be saved by a straw.

Boy I believe in anything that might save me from the gallows.

Calm Woman Whatever the cost?

Boy I'm to lose my life. What is worth more than that?

Calm Woman Your soul maybe.

Boy My soul?

Calm Woman A poor thing, no doubt, but at this moment the best you have to offer.

Boy Would it be enough?

Calm Woman For what?

Boy Would he save me?

Calm Woman Who is he?

Boy You know who.

Calm Woman Do I?

Boy Your—master.

Calm Woman His name?

Boy The devil.

There is a disconcerted reaction from the other prisoners—part shock, but part discomfort at the nearness of his reply to their own thoughts

Calm Woman That's better. Before a contract each party should be aware of the other's identity.
Boy Would the devil take it?
Girl Think, lad.
Boy What of?
Girl Such dealings may be right enough for that one. She made her choice and must surely abide by it.
Calm Woman True. Not many have cheated the devil.
Girl I think there be many the devil have cheated.
Neat Woman Aye. Father of lies.
Old Woman God save us.
Boy Offer me a chance as frail as a baby's hair, and I'll cling to it.
Girl Parting with your soul's a powerful step.
Boy What's a soul without a body?
Girl But to be damned, lad . . . Think on the burning, fiery lake of brimstone.
Calm Woman Think of tomorrow's scaffold and the newly-dug, waiting grave.
Girl Lady, you tempt like the devil himself. Were you sent to prison here to bargain for souls?
Calm Woman No offer has been made on either side.
Neat Woman Souls cannot be bought and sold.
Calm Woman They have been offered before now. Maybe accepted.
Man Like so many yards of linsey-woolsey? The devil doesn't stand market.
Calm Woman Where's the need? Customers seek him out.
Old Woman Our Father, which art in . . . (*She subsides, mumbling*)
Girl That's right, grandmother. Pray. Drown that wicked tempting.
Boy I asked—would he save me?
Girl From what, laddie? From dying? The devil can never save you from that. Late or soon everybody has to die. Even me. I suppose.

Boy Everybody doesn't die with halters round their necks. What must I do? To—to offer.

Old Woman Pray, boy. Lead us not into temptation. Pray.

Boy Pray for yourself, old mumbletooth.

Old Woman Lead him not, Lord. Into temptation, Lord.

Neat Woman But if there should be hope.

Man There is no hope. Only that, in the after-life, we may look down from our green pastures—and see our enemy frying for eternity. As he will. As he must if there is any divine justice. The covetous misbegotten whose greed brought me to this pass. The kind neighbour who denounced me. Let me hear him scream in the infernal fire. I can hope for that. (*Although he starts the speech in a matter-of-fact tone, he now finds himself ranting, and pulls himself together*) You are driving me as mad as yourself with this talk of hope.

Neat Woman There must be hope. They can always admit their mistake. A reprieve would be so easy—even at the gallows foot. A piece of paper. A pardon.

Boy Yes. Yes. A mere stroke of the pen.

Man Now you've roused him again.

Boy No miracles needed. No angels . . .

Calm Woman Or devils?

Boy With flaming swords to open prison doors. A goose quill might do it.

Man That stroke would be more of a miracle than a flaming sword.

Neat Woman She can control hearts and minds. An idea placed. The idea moves the mind. The mind moves the hand. The hand moves the pen . . .

Boy A pardon!

Man You're maundering.

Neat Woman If the lad might be saved, then I might be saved.

Man You?

Neat Woman It is possible.

Calm Woman Anything is possible.

Neat Woman You truly have the power to control minds?

Calm Woman Given time, place and circumstance.

Man Equivocation. If she can do so much, why was she tried with us, found guilty with us, condemned with us?

Calm Woman Because time, place and circumstance were not conjoined.

Man Mummery.

Calm Woman I can only use such power as flows through me.

Man And for that you're at the beck of your so-called master.

Calm Woman Come daylight all questions will be answered.

Neat Woman Come daylight we shall be—we shall—we . . .

Calm Woman Is that light in the sky entirely the moon? Could it be false dawn?

Neat Woman Don't dangle promises then turn away.

Calm Woman I promised nothing.

Old Woman Deliver us from evil. I have always walked in the sight of The Lord.

Neat Woman You can afford to be virtuous. All but a few of your days are behind you. What have you to lose if you are buried tomorrow?

Old Woman The last few drops in the bottle are the most precious.

Man She's a woman and a prisoner. No more, no less. She can't help herself, let alone you.

Boy Lady, forget those squabbling jays and help me.

Neat Woman Help me.

Calm Woman Do I understand you are both offering yourselves?

Boy For my life.

Neat Woman For my freedom.

Calm Woman Haggle later over what your small change may buy. But you are offering . . .

Boy Aye.

Neat Woman Aye.

Man Aye.

Calm Woman You, too?

Man If they escape, why should I be left to suffer?

Old Woman Or I?

Calm Woman You, goody?

Old Woman I've a life to lose.

Calm Woman Greedy. After all you've had.

Old Woman A week. A day. An hour more. I'd pay all I own.

Calm Woman Money's no longer legal tender here.

Neat Woman Take whatever is needful.

Boy Take anything.

Man Take it.

Old Woman Mine, too.

Calm Woman The saint a devil would be.

Man Sneer. Gloat. We surrender to—to—whatever you surrendered to.

Neat Woman The Dark Powers.

Old Woman The—Other One.

Boy Satan.

Girl Lad!

Boy Let me be.

Girl Dying means nothing to me, because I can't think of myself as dead. But there's a darkness blacker than night. And I'm afraid of that.

Boy There's no darkness deeper than the grave.

Girl There is. There is. Like the black mire that sucks down creatures, never to be seen again. I've seen poor sheep lost so. I wouldn't have you stumble into the like of that.

Boy My mind is made up. Let the ceremony begin.

Calm Woman Ceremony?

Neat Woman Surely unholy rites are necessary.

Man Teach us the words.

Old Woman The Lord's Prayer backwards. The witch way. Isn't that so?

Neat Woman What circles and pentagrams must be described?

Girl I won't listen. I won't listen.

Calm Woman You wouldn't understand, would you, if I assured you that such performances are unnecessary?

Neat Woman Hurry. Whatever is done must be completed before dawn.

Calm Woman You need only make a pact in your hearts.

Man Surely there must be words.

Old Woman In Latin.

Calm Woman The devil understands your mother tongue.

Neat Woman And blood. Shouldn't blood be spilled?

Calm Woman If it is to be, then it will be.

Boy Begin. Begin. The words, madam, please.

Calm Woman The North wind doth blow, and we shall have snow.

Man You choose a perilous moment for jesting, lady.

Calm Woman I tell you again—intent is all that counts. Words are no more than outward form. If you would truly give yourself to the devil, then you have already given yourself to the devil.

Neat Woman Without words, how can we tell what has been given or taken?

Calm Woman The damned have no doubts.

Man But *we* do. The words.

Boy Sounds.

Neat Woman Incantations.

Calm Woman So be it. You will cry, "Come Satan."

Neat Woman Come Satan. Is that all?

Calm Woman Simple and to the point. And you, "Here, Satan."

Man Here, Satan? I'd employ more ceremony in calling a dog.

Calm Woman He'll understand. "To us, Satan."

Old Woman To us, Satan.

Calm Woman Will you remember that?

Old Woman To us, Satan. To us, Satan. To us, Satan.

Calm Woman Repeat the message until you have it by heart.

Boy And I?

Girl No!

Boy My share.

Calm Woman "Now, Satan."

Boy Now, Satan.

Girl No, lad.

The Calm Woman points to each in turn. They repeat their lines

Neat Woman Come, Satan.

Man Here, Satan.

Old Woman To us, Satan.

Boy Now, Satan. Are we to move?

Calm Woman Surely.

Man To dance?

Calm Woman As the fit seizes you.

Old Woman Widdershins.

Calm Woman So much occult lore at your fingertips, granny? Fie, you've been hoodwinking me.

Old Woman I kenned it general knowledge.

Calm Woman Who am I to deny the power of tradition? Dance widdershins, then. Raise your voice. Clap hands. Clank your chains. Make a joyful noise before the Dark Ones. (*She turns from them and looks through the window*)

Boy No more than that?

Calm Woman A cloud threatens the moon. Strange. When I last looked the sky was clear.

Man Shall we begin?

Calm Woman A cloud risen from nowhere.

Neat Woman Shall we . . . ?

Calm Woman Aye. Begin. I foresee the outcome. A stranger might laugh at the joke. To trade so much for so little. In your own time. Begin.

The four are sheepish and embarrassed, unsure of themselves

Do you call on me to be choirmaster, too? This is your invocation, not mine. Oh, very well. You there.

Neat Woman (*nervously*) Come, Satan.

Calm Woman You.

Man Here, Satan.

Calm Woman And you.

Old Woman To us, Satan.

Calm Woman And?

Boy Now, Satan.

Calm Woman (*turning from them to the window again*) Round and round the maypole.

They recite the incantation again and again, moving uncertainly round in a circle. As they repeat the words and movements, conviction grows. They clap and stamp and shout, affected by the rhythm. For a while the Girl watches them fascinated, but with growing apprehension, until she can contain herself no longer

Girl (*over the chanting*) Stop. Please stop. Now, please. You mustn't raise the devil. It's a sin. You'll be damned. I don't want to be damned with you. Stop them somebody. They're calling the devil. If he should come . . . Face to face. Like a roaring lion. Seeking to devour. Stop.

The dancers are now reaching a climax in a self-induced trance, shouting and waving their arms

(*Shouting*) Gaoler! Stop them. (*She beats on the door*) Gaoler. Hark. Your prisoners are escaping. Stop them. Help me. Help. Help.

As the sound of the Girl penetrates their hysteria, the dancers falter and pause. Their voices die away. They look about, bemused, as though just awakened. The Man drags the Girl from the door

Man Vixen.
Old Woman What? Where?
Boy We—faltered.
Neat Woman I could feel A Presence.
Boy He was near.
Neat Woman Approaching.
Old Woman Why did we pause?
Man Ask that mudlark.
Girl It's a sin.
Man On our heads be it.
Boy I heard swooping wings. A distant voice. Pounding like a great heart.
Man You could hear this lump assaulting the door.
Old Woman I remembered the words.
Man Try again.
Girl Summon the Evil One, and I'll drive him back.
Man I'll stop your blabber mouth.

As he rounds on the Girl, she aims a blow at his middle

Girl I learned how to strike and where to strike. How else could a maid keep her virtue among men like animals?
Boy We'd never wish to hurt you. Leave us to our own way.
Girl To the everlasting fire?
Neat Woman So little time. Every minute lost could be the one needful.
Man Again then. Here Satan.
Old Woman Eh? Oh. To us, Satan.
Calm Woman The cloud advances like a giant hand prepared to seize the moon.
Neat Woman Come, Satan.
Man Here, Satan.
Old Woman To us, Satan.
Boy Now, Satan.

They repeat their lines circling, but keeping a wary eye on the Girl. Next time round the Girl interjects between each of their lines—at first softly, but growing louder. They become louder and faster in an attempt to drown her voice until they are all shouting. The glances directed at the Girl progress from irritation to anger to fury

Neat Woman Come, Satan.
Girl Our Father.
Man Here, Satan.
Girl Which art in Heaven.
Old Woman To us, Satan.
Girl Hallowed be thy name.
Boy Now, Satan.
Girl Thy Kingdom come . . .
Neat Woman Come, Satan.
Girl Thy will be done.
Man Here, Satan.
Girl On earth.
Old Woman To us, Satan.
Girl As it is in Heaven.
Boy Now, Satan.
Girl Give us this day.
Neat Woman Come, Satan.
Girl Our daily bread.
Man Here, Satan.
Girl Forgive us our trespasses.
Old Woman To us, Satan.
Girl As we forgive them . . .
Boy Now, Satan.
Girl That trespass against us.
Neat Woman Come, Satan.
Girl Deliver us from evil.
Man Here, Satan.
Girl For thine is the kingdom.
Old Woman To us, Satan.
Girl The power and the glory.
Boy Now, Satan.
Girl For ever and ever.

As their voices reach a crescendo a cloud covers the moon. Darkness.

Amen. Aaaaaaaaaaah!

There is a scuffle in the darkness

Calm Woman Like a great bat swooping upon the moon. A cloud. No more than a cloud. It passes.

Light floods into the cell as the moon shines again. The Man has the chain of his fetters pulled tightly across the Girl's throat. After a few seconds he releases her and the body drops to the ground

Old Woman Is the ceremony over?
Man She interfered.
Boy Her eyes.
Man Cover her with straw.

They drag the body to the back of the cell and pile straw on it

Calm Woman No pity. No remorse. What had to be done has been done.
Man She would have died tomorrow anyway.
Neat Woman Today. Today.
Boy But shall we? Where's the reply?
Calm Woman In your heart.
Boy There's nothing in my heart but a great emptiness. Where is. the devil?
Calm Woman Look where I told you.
Man These are riddles on top of riddles.
Calm Woman You can solve them as well as I.
Boy How are we to be saved?
Calm Woman Saved? That word's a riddle in itself. I shall not hang. That is certain. (*She laughs gently*)
Neat Woman You knew that much before.
Calm Woman But not the why. Not the how. Now the picture is complete. Oh, infernal majesty's an artist in drawing up a contract. (*She laughs*)
Man You are to escape the gallows, but what of us?
Boy We performed all that you bade us.
Old Woman I remembered the words.
Boy The ceremony was complete.
Neat Woman Even to blood shedding.
Man What now?
Calm Woman Well—the devil may have accepted your offering. When all's said and done a soul's a soul, no matter how flawed.
Man But where's the sign?
Calm Woman A dead girl under the straw.
Boy How will the devil keep his promise to us?
Calm Woman Promise? What promise?

Boy We made a bargain.
Neat Woman It was agreed.
Calm Woman I promised nothing. You offered your souls.
Boy For our lives.
Man We killed for them.
Old Woman What is the argument about?
Neat Woman We delivered to him.
Boy We paid.
Calm Woman I paid.
Man What was your price?
Calm Woman You.
Old Woman I can't make out her words. Or if I heard, they didn't make sense.
Man They don't make sense.
Calm Woman No?
Boy Will the devil deliver us?
Calm Woman Should he pay for what was his already?
Boy His?
Calm Woman Look to your heart, I said. You turned to Hell before you turned to me.
Neat Woman We gained nothing?
Calm Woman Nothing.
Neat Woman We risked our souls for nothing?
Old Woman No!
Calm Woman Pray, granny. Pray for them. Pray for yourself.
Old Woman I—I . . . Words are a jumble inside my head. I'm confused. (*She huddles mumbling in a corner*)
Man Shall we not escape this place?
Calm Woman No.
Man Cheat.
Calm Woman How so? You may not have given yourselves to hell when the judge condemned you. But you'll hang as witches —and justice will have been done. On four lost souls. (*She laughs. Her laughter grows. She turns her back on the Man*)
Man (*with a despairing cry*) Fiend.

The Man raises his manacled fists and brings them down on the neck of the Calm Woman. Her laughter is cut short and she crumples. The Boy and the Neat Woman kick the prone body

Boy Deceiver.

Neat Woman Liar.

They kick again and again, until their fury passes. The Boy kneels down beside the body

Boy She—she won't die on the gallows.
Neat Woman Dead?
Boy Dead.
Man She goaded me. She forced me.
Boy The devil kept his promise to her.
Man Aye. She'll be with him now. Burning. In fires everlasting. Well, at least we escaped damnation. Satan spurned us. Or our cries failed to reach him. Perhaps for the best. When the guards come, we'll make a brave show on the scaffold.

With a cry the Boy throws himself to the ground and lies whimpering

Runt. We shall ascend to glory. We shall look down from our green pastures and behold that fallen woman shrieking in eternal torment.
Neat Woman Pray that it be so. Pray for us, goody.
Old Woman The words. The words.
Neat Woman Try.
Old Woman Ever and ever.
Man The wrong end, fumble-wits. That's the way witches pray.
Old Woman Ever and ever. Help me. Please. Help me to pray.
Neat Woman For glory the.
Man No, no. It should be—the power the kingdom—

The Boy sits up open-mouthed

Old Woman —the is thine for evil from us deliver—
Boy Damned. We're damned!
Man
Old Woman } —but temptation into not us lead { (*Speaking*
Neat Woman } us against trespass that . . . { *together*)

The Boy's screams drown their words, as—

the CURTAIN *falls*

FURNITURE AND PROPERTY LIST

On stage: Bench
Low rostrum, or second bench
Straw

Personal: CAST: 6 sets of manacles

LIGHTING PLOT

Property fittings required: nil
Interior. A prison cell
To open: Night. Effect of moonlight streaming through
              barred window
Cue 1   **Girl:** "For ever and ever."   (Page 15)
              All lighting dims as cloud passes across moon
Cue 2   **Calm Woman:** "It passes."   (Page 15)
              Return to previous lighting

CPSIA information can be obtained at www.ICGtesting.com
Printed in the USA
LVOW07s1816260815

451630LV00030B/1165/P

9 780573 120022